Daily Reflections and Stories for Children

Book 2
Stories of 'Abdu'l-Bahá

compiled by
Munirih Hodge and Margo Styan

illustrated by
Margo Styan

GEORGE RONALD
OXFORD

George Ronald, *Publisher*
Oxford
www.grbooks.com

© Munirih Hodge and Margo Styan 2011
Illustrations © Margo Styan
Reprinted 2013

All Rights Reserved

*A catalogue record for this book is available
from the British Library*

ISBN 978-0-85398-552-5

CONTENTS

Preface
Acknowledgements

1. Detachment: *Left with Nothing*
2. Love: *The Dungeon*
3. Protection: *A Son's Love*
4. Self-Sacrifice: *Little Sleep*
5. Steadfastness: *The Most Great Prison*
6. Patience: *Stolen Coal*
7. Understanding: *Death of a Child*
8. Sincerity: *Good For Business?*
9. Compassion: *Without a Bed*
10. Helpfulness: *Looking for a Father*
11. Generosity: *Cloaks for Everyone!*
12. Selflessness: *A New Car*
13. Courtesy: *No Appointment*
14. Loving-Kindness: *Fruitful Trees*
15. Divinity: *Power Within*
16. Humbleness: *Crystal Water*
17. Joy: *Finding Laughter*
18. Charity: *Christmas Eve*
19. Humility: *'Abdu'l-Bahá Becomes a Knight*

Bibliography
References

No name, no title, no mention, no commendation hath he nor will ever have except 'Abdu'l-Bahá. This is my longing. This is my supreme apex. This is my greatest yearning. This is my eternal life. This is my everlasting glory![i]

PREFACE

by Enayat Rawhani

Bahá'u'lláh chose His eldest son, 'Abdu'l-Bahá, as His successor and asked all the Bahá'í's to turn to Him for guidance and example. He said that 'Abdu'l-Bahá was the perfect believer whose behaviour exemplified the noblest human qualities and the most cherished Bahá'í ideals. He referred to 'Abdu'l-Bahá as the Master and the Centre of His Covenant. He said 'Abdu'l-Bahá was the Mystery of God among us. This means that in 'Abdu'l-Bahá we can see a harmonious blend of human and divine qualities.

'Abdu'l-Bahá was the essence of purity. He was devoted to God and committed to the service of humanity. He spent His days serving God, Bahá'u'lláh and humanity. Although Bahá'u'lláh had given Him great names and titles, 'Abdu'l-Bahá begged Bahá'u'lláh to grant Him the wish to be His most humble servant. He then asked friends to call Him 'Abdu'l-Bahá. He said,

> My name is 'Abdu'l-Bahá [which means the Servant of Glory], my identity is 'Abdu'l-Bahá, my qualification is 'Abdu'l-Bahá, my reality is 'Abdu'l-Bahá, my praise is 'Abdu'l-Bahá, Thraldom to the Blessed Perfection is my glorious refulgent diadem; and servitude to all the human race is my perpetual religion.[ii]

We should learn more about 'Abdu'l-Bahá and follow in His footsteps.

ACKNOWLEDGEMENTS

We would like to thank Margo's children for inspiring this project many years ago, and Munirih's daughters, whose eagerness and enthusiasm to pick a daily reflection each night encouraged us to continue. To Pixie MacCallum we extend our heartfelt gratitude for her invaluable input and feedback and to Dan Hodge and Jim Styan we are eternally grateful for their unwavering assistance and support.

Thank you Enayat Rawhani for capturing the essence of 'Abdu'l-Bahá so eloquently in the Preface. And our deepest appreciation to Jacqueline Mehrabi for her permission to adapt and print the stories 'Fruitful Trees', first published by *Dayspring Magazine*, and 'Death of a Child', which originally appeared under the title 'The Gift' in *Stories of 'Abdu'l-Bahá*. Our sincerest gratitude to George Ronald, Publisher for having confidence in our vision and encapsulating our intention for this book so impeccably.

1
DETACHMENT

Say: God sufficeth all things above all things, and nothing in the heavens or in the earth but God sufficeth. Verily, He is in Himself the Knower, the Sustainer, the Omnipotent.[1]

O Son of Being! If poverty overtake thee, be not sad; for in time the Lord of wealth shall visit thee. Fear not abasement, for glory shall one day rest on thee.[2]

Left with Nothing

In 1852 two half-crazed Bábís tried to kill the King of Persia. The other Bábís were wrongly held responsible for the attack and the officials took 'Abdu'l-Bahá's father, Bahá'u'lláh, to prison. 'Abdu'l-Bahá was only eight years old.

People came into their house and stole all their belongings. All their possessions and land were taken away. Overnight 'Abdu'l-Bahá went from living a life of luxury to having nothing, not even enough food. There was no bread to eat and He was very hungry. His mother poured some flour into the palm of His hand. 'Abdu'l-Bahá ate the flour instead of bread.[3]

2
LOVE

O God! Rear this little babe in the bosom of Thy love, and give it milk from the breast of Thy Providence. Cultivate this fresh plant in the rose garden of Thy love and aid it to grow through the showers of Thy bounty. Make it a child of the kingdom, and lead it to Thy heavenly realm. Thou art powerful and kind, and Thou art the Bestower, the Generous, the Lord of surpassing bounty.[4]

O Son of Man! If thou lovest Me, turn away from thyself; and if thou seekest My pleasure, regard not thine own; that thou mayest die in Me and I may eternally live in thee.[5]

The Dungeon

Bahá'u'lláh was imprisoned in a dark, smelly dungeon when 'Abdu'l-Bahá was only eight years old. The prisoners in the dungeon sat huddled together in one cell with their feet in stocks and chains around their necks. They sat on a floor covered in dirt and filled with bugs and rats. No light was allowed in the dungeon to warm the icy coldness the prisoners felt.

'Abdu'l-Bahá loved His father very much and desperately wanted to see Him. A servant took 'Abdu'l-Bahá to see His father. When 'Abdu'l-Bahá entered the prison the wardens pointed to the cell holding Bahá'u'lláh. The servant carried 'Abdu'l-Bahá on his shoulders.

'I saw a dark, steep place,' 'Abdu'l-Bahá said later as He talked of His visit to the dungeon.

They entered a small, narrow doorway, and went down two steps, but after the steps they could see nothing. When they were in the middle of the stairway, all of a sudden they heard Bahá'u'lláh's voice.

'Do not bring him in here,' He said.

The servant took 'Abdu'l-Bahá back. They sat outside waiting for the prisoners to come out. Finally Bahá'u'lláh was brought out of the dungeon. He was chained to several other prisoners. The chain was so heavy the prisoners moved it along with great difficulty. 'Abdu'l-Bahá was happy to see His father but deeply saddened and heartbroken to see Him in this way.[6]

3
PROTECTION

Keep them ever in safety beneath Thine all-protecting eye. Assist them to exalt Thy Word; make Thou their hearts to be constant in Thy love; strengthen Thou their backs that they may serve Thee well; in servitude, strengthen Thou their powers.

Spread Thou through them Thy sweet savours far and wide; expound through them Thy Holy Writ; make known through them Thine Utterance; fulfil through them Thy Words; through them pour out Thy mercy.

Thou art verily the Mighty, the Powerful. Thou art verily the Clement, the Compassionate.[7]

Today, the Lord of Hosts is the defender of the Covenant, the forces of the Kingdom protect it, heavenly souls tender their services, and heavenly angels promulgate and spread it broadcast.[8]

A Son's Love

After four months Bahá'u'lláh was released from the dungeon and was sent to Baghdad. When 'Abdu'l-Bahá was nearly ten years old Bahá'u'lláh left Baghdad and went into the mountains. Bahá'u'lláh lived as a dervish, a poor man dressed in rags wishing to meditate and pray alone. 'Abdu'l-Bahá was deeply attached to His father. After He left 'Abdu'l-Bahá became miserable. He would go away by Himself for hours and when others went to look for Him, often they would find Him crying.

'Abdu'l-Bahá was an unusual child. He did not like to play and amuse Himself like other children. Instead He spent time memorizing all the Báb's writings. He would not go to school or try to study. He loved horse riding and was a very talented and skilful horseman.

After two years Bahá'u'lláh came down from the mountains. 'Abdu'l-Bahá was extremely happy to have His father home.

Once Bahá'u'lláh was back in Baghdad many people came to hear His teachings. But some came only out of curiosity and caused trouble. Since Bahá'u'lláh wished only to see those interested in His teachings 'Abdu'l-Bahá decided to protect His father from intruders. He prepared two signs. On the door to His own room He put one sign, which read, 'Those who come for information may apply within; those who come only because of curiosity had better stay away'. He put the other sign on His father's room: 'Let those who are searching for God come, and come, and come.' Then He announced He would be the first person to see anyone coming to see His father. If a person were a true seeker He permitted him to see His father; if not, 'Abdu'l-Bahá did not let him in.[9]

4
SELF-SACRIFICE

May my spirit be a sacrifice to the wrongs Thou didst suffer, and my soul be a ransom for the adversities Thou didst sustain. I beseech God, by Thee and by them whose faces have been illumined with the splendours of the light of Thy countenance, and who, for love of Thee, have observed all whereunto they were bidden, to remove the veils that have come in between Thee and Thy creatures, and to supply me with the good of this world and the world to come. Thou art, in truth, the Almighty, the Most Exalted, the All-Glorious, the Ever-Forgiving, the Most Compassionate.[10]

O servant of Bahá! Be self-sacrificing in the path of God, and wing thy flight unto the heavens of the love of the Abhá Beauty, for any movement animated by love moveth from the periphery to the centre, from space to the Day-Star of the universe.[11]

Little Sleep

The Governor of Turkey had great respect for Bahá'u'lláh. But finally, in March 1863, the Governor gave in to the continual demands from the Turkish government to have Bahá'u'lláh removed from Baghdad. The Governor invited Bahá'u'lláh and His family to leave Baghdad and go to Constantinople.

Bahá'u'lláh's friends were deeply saddened by the approaching separation from Him. 'Abdu'l-Bahá therefore made arrangements for His father to go to a beautiful garden, the Garden of Riḍván, to spend time with the friends before leaving for Constantinople. During this time Bahá'u'lláh told 'Abdu'l-Bahá He was the messenger from God the Báb had promised. From this moment on 'Abdu'l-Bahá made Himself the body-guard and servant of His father. He guarded Him day and night on their journey to Constantinople.

'Abdu'l-Bahá rode by Bahá'u'lláh's wagon and watched Him near His tent. He had very little sleep and because He was young He became weak. His horse was a fine Arabian, wild and spirited. No one was able to mount 'Abdu'l-Bahá's horse except Him. To get a little rest 'Abdu'l-Bahá would ride swiftly, quite a distance ahead of the travellers. He would then dismount, lay the horse down, throw Himself on the ground and place His head on His horse's neck. He would sleep until the procession came up. His horse would awaken Him with a nudge and 'Abdu'l-Bahá would remount. This continued for the three months it took to get to Constantinople.[12]

5
STEADFASTNESS

Direct, then, his eyes, O my God, towards the horizon of Thy loving-kindness, and make steadfast his heart in its attachment to Thee, and unloose his tongue to praise Thee, and make him able to hold fast the cord of Thy love, and to cling to the hem of Thy bounteousness, and to proclaim Thy name amidst Thy creatures, and to recount Thy virtues throughout Thy realm, in such wise that no obstacle will deter him from turning to Thy name, the All-Bountiful, and no veil shut him out from Thee, in Whose hand is the dominion of utterance and the kingdom of all names and attributes! . . . [13]

Verily the Abhá Beauty made a promise to the beloved who are steadfast in the Covenant, that He would reinforce their strivings with the strongest of supports, and succour them with His triumphant might.[14]

The Most Great Prison

Bahá'u'lláh, 'Abdu'l-Bahá and the family lived in Constantinople for about three and a half months. Then they were sent to Adrianople, where they lived for almost five years. On 12 August 1868 Bahá'u'lláh and His family were banished from Adrianople. They first went to Gallipoli and then were sent to 'Akká. 'Abdu'l-Bahá was 24 years old. There were about 70 people, family and friends who climbed onto the ship at Gallipoli bound for Haifa. 'Akká was across the bay from Haifa. When they reached Haifa they all got off the ship and climbed into small sailing boats to travel to 'Akká. Once they arrived in 'Akká there was no place to dock the boats. The only way to get to shore was to climb out of the boats and wade to the land. The Governor ordered the men to carry the women on their backs. 'Abdu'l-Bahá did not agree with the Governor's order. Instead He was one of the first to get to the shore. He found a chair and, with the help of another man, carried the women ashore in it.

It was the last day of August, the middle of summer and extremely hot when they landed beneath the gloomy walls of 'Akká. 'Akká was a prison city where only the worst criminals were sent. When the Bahá'ís arrived in 'Akká Bahá'u'lláh decided to call it the 'Most Great Prison'. The air smelled terrible and the water and the streets stank. When the Bahá'ís entered the barracks huge doors were closed and bolted behind them. They were led to a room, walking through mud almost as high as their ankles. There was nowhere to sit or lie down.

The first night they were not given any food or water. They even begged for water but no one gave them any. Very soon the diseased air of 'Akká and the unhealthy state of the place began to affect them. Everyone, except two people, got very sick. Three died. 'Abdu'l-Bahá took care of the sick. He washed, fed and nursed them. He protected His father and faced the rudeness and anger of the people who lived in 'Akká. He held His ground against the brutal and cruel guards and officials. He never gave up.[15]

6
PATIENCE

Help them through Thy strengthening grace, I beseech Thee, O my God, to suffer patiently in their love for Thee, and unveil to their eyes what Thou hast decreed for them behind the Tabernacle of Thine unfailing protection, so that they may rush forward to meet what is preordained for them in Thy path, and may vie in hasting after tribulation in their love towards Thee . . . Powerful art Thou to do what Thou willest. No God is there but Thee, the Omniscient, the All-Wise.[16]

O Son of Man! For everything there is a sign. The sign of love is fortitude under My decree and patience under My trials.[17]

Stolen Coal

'Abdu'l-Bahá and His family lived in the prison city of 'Akká. 'Abdu'l-Bahá quickly became friends with many people and helped them whenever He could.

Once a Bahá'í needed charcoal to heat his house but the people in 'Akká would not sell it to him because his religious beliefs were different from theirs. 'Abdu'l-Bahá got permission to send out of the city for charcoal and a camel-load was brought back. The driver of the camel stopped by the shop of a Christian merchant.

'This is better charcoal than I can get,' the merchant said and decided to take it for himself.

When 'Abdu'l-Bahá heard what happened to the charcoal He went to the merchant's shop and stood in the doorway. The merchant did not notice 'Abdu'l-Bahá so 'Abdu'l-Bahá entered and sat down by the door. The merchant ignored Him and continued doing business with others coming to the store. 'Abdu'l-Bahá waited in silence for three hours. Finally everyone left and no one else came into the store.

'Are you one of those prisoners here?' asked the merchant. 'What have you done that you are imprisoned?'

'Since you ask me,' replied 'Abdu'l-Bahá, 'I will tell you. We have done nothing. We are persecuted as Christ was persecuted.'

'What do you know of Christ?' asked the merchant.

'Abdu'l-Bahá replied in such a way that the merchant could see 'Abdu'l-Bahá knew a lot about Christ and the Christian Bible. The merchant then began questioning Him about the Bible and was very interested in what 'Abdu'l-Bahá had to say.

Then the merchant invited 'Abdu'l-Bahá to sit beside him and they continued talking for two hours. At the end of their conversation the merchant was very pleased.

'The coal is gone, I cannot return it to you, but here is the money,' the merchant said.

He walked 'Abdu'l-Bahá to the door and down into the street, treating Him with great respect.[18]

7

UNDERSTANDING

O Thou compassionate Lord, Thou Who art generous and able! We are servants of Thine sheltered beneath Thy providence. Cast Thy glance of favour upon us. Give light to our eyes, hearing to our ears, and understanding and love to our hearts. Render our souls joyous and happy through Thy glad tidings . . . O God! Unite us and connect our hearts with Thy indissoluble bond. Verily, Thou art the Giver, Thou art the Kind One and Thou art the Almighty.[19]

O thou beloved maid-servant of God, although the loss of a son is indeed heart-breaking and beyond the limits of human endurance, yet one who knoweth and understandeth is assured that the son hath not been lost but, rather, hath stepped from this world into another, and she will find him in the divine realm. That reunion shall be for eternity, while in this world separation is inevitable and bringeth with it a burning grief.[20]

Death of a Child

'Abdu'l-Bahá had a son called Ḥusayn. When Ḥusayn was five years old he became very ill and died. Some Arabs living in the city of 'Akká came to 'Abdu'l-Bahá to say how sorry they were that His son had died.

'Abdu'l-Bahá smiled at them and asked them if they thought God was generous.

'Yes, indeed,' said the men. 'He has given us everything.'

Then 'Abdu'l-Bahá asked them if they thought a generous man would give something then take it away again.

'Of course not!' said the men in surprise.

'Abdu'l-Bahá explained to them that God was generous when He gave Him a little son, and He did not take His son away. God was just keeping His son for Him.[21]

8
SINCERITY

O God! Make this assemblage radiant. Make the hearts merciful. Confer the bounties of the Holy Spirit. Endow them with a power from heaven. Bless them with heavenly minds. Increase their sincerity, so that with all humility and contrition they may turn to Thy kingdom and be occupied with service to the world of humanity. May each one become a radiant candle. May each one become a brilliant star. May each one become beautiful in colour and redolent of fragrance in the kingdom of God . . .

O God! Endow us with Thy providence. Thou art the Powerful. Thou art the Giver. Thou art the Beneficent.[22]

We should at all times manifest our truthfulness and sincerity, nay rather, we must be constant in our faithfulness and trustworthiness, and occupy ourselves in offering prayers for the good of all.[23]

Good For Business?

'Abdu'l-Bahá and a group of people were all travelling together, some walking and some riding their animals. Included in the group was a merchant. On the way to their destination they stopped in a village. Many people gathered around 'Abdu'l-Bahá wanting to meet Him and talk to Him. When it was time for the travellers to resume their journey they mounted their animals or continued walking with the group. A while later they stopped in a town. The same thing happened: people surrounded 'Abdu'l-Bahá. This occurred again when they stopped in the next village. The merchant travelling with 'Abdu'l-Bahá noticed the obvious love and respect shown to 'Abdu'l-Bahá. He took 'Abdu'l-Bahá aside and told Him he wished to become a Bahá'í.

'Abdu'l-Bahá asked him why he wanted to become a Bahá'í.

'You are a Bahá'í,' the merchant replied, 'and wherever you go, great crowds of people flock out to meet you, while no one comes to meet me; so I wish to become a Bahá'í.'

'Abdu'l-Bahá asked if this were the real reason.

'I also think it will help my business, as I will have all these people come to meet me,' answered the merchant without any shame in his voice.

'Do not become a Bahá'í,' 'Abdu'l-Bahá told him frankly. 'It is better for you to remain as you are.'[24]

9

COMPASSION

O compassionate God! Thanks be to Thee for Thou hast awakened and made me conscious. Thou hast given me a seeing eye and favoured me with a hearing ear, hast led me to Thy kingdom and guided me to Thy path. Thou hast shown me the right way and caused me to enter the ark of deliverance. O God! Keep me steadfast and make me firm and staunch. Protect me from violent tests and preserve and shelter me in the strongly fortified fortress of Thy Covenant and Testament. Thou art the Powerful. Thou art the Seeing. Thou art the Hearing.

O Thou the Compassionate God. Bestow upon me a heart which, like unto a glass, may be illumined with the light of Thy love, and confer upon me thoughts which may change this world into a rose garden through the outpourings of heavenly grace.

Thou art the Compassionate, the Merciful. Thou art the Great Beneficent God.[25]

Be compassionate, so that your actions will shine like unto the light streaming forth from the lamp.[26]

Without a Bed

When 'Abdu'l-Bahá lived in 'Akká His room often did not have a bed in it. He was constantly giving His bed to the poor and needy. Wrapped in a blanket, 'Abdu'l-Bahá would sleep on the floor or even on the roof of His home. It was not possible to buy a bed in the town of 'Akká. A new bed had to be ordered from Haifa and it took at least 36 hours to arrive.

One morning when 'Abdu'l-Bahá was doing His normal round of visits He found a feverish person tossing on the bare ground. He immediately sent him His bed. It was only after a kind friend accidentally found out 'Abdu'l-Bahá no longer had a bed that 'Abdu'l-Bahá received another one.[27]

10

HELPFULNESS

O Thou kind Lord! These lovely children are the handiwork of the fingers of Thy might and the wondrous signs of Thy greatness. O God! Protect these children, graciously assist them to be educated and enable them to render service to the world of humanity. O God! These children are pearls, cause them to be nurtured within the shell of Thy loving-kindness.

Thou art the Bountiful, the All-Loving.[28]

Be ye loving fathers to the orphan, and a refuge to the helpless, and a treasury for the poor, and a cure for the ailing. Be ye the helpers of every victim of oppression, the patrons of the disadvantaged. Think ye at all times of rendering some service to every member of the human race. Pay ye no heed to aversion and rejection, to disdain, hostility, injustice: act ye in the opposite way. Be ye sincerely kind, not in appearance only.[29]

Looking for a Father

A Turkish man, living in Haifa, lost his job. He and his wife and children became very poor and were in desperate need of food and clothing. They went to 'Abdu'l-Bahá and asked for His assistance and 'Abdu'l-Bahá helped them greatly.

When the poor man became ill, again 'Abdu'l-Bahá was ready to help. He provided a doctor, medicine and necessities to make him comfortable.

When this man felt he was going to die, he asked 'Abdu'l-Bahá to come to his house. He also called his children to join them.

'Here', he told the children, 'is your father, who will take care of you when I am gone.'

One morning four small children arrived at the home of 'Abdu'l-Bahá and announced, 'We want our father!'

'Abdu'l-Bahá, hearing their voices, knew who they were. With deep sadness they told Him that their father had died.

'Abdu'l-Bahá brought them into His home and gave them something to drink and sweets and cakes to eat. He then went with them to their house. It turned out that their father had fainted and was not dead. But, unfortunately, the next day he did die.

'Abdu'l-Bahá arranged for the funeral and provided food, clothing and travel-tickets for the family to go to Turkey.[30]

11

GENEROSITY

O Thou kind Lord! O Thou Who art generous and merciful! We are the servants of Thy threshold and are gathered beneath the sheltering shadow of Thy divine unity. The sun of Thy mercy is shining upon all, and the clouds of Thy bounty shower upon all. Thy gifts encompass all, Thy loving providence sustains all, Thy protection overshadows all, and the glances of Thy favour are cast upon all . . .

Thou art the Giver, the Merciful, the Omnipotent.[31]

―

O Son of Man! Deny not My servant should he ask anything from thee, for his face is My face; be then abashed before Me.[32]

Cloaks for Everyone!

In the winter in 'Akká the poor would suffer much more than in the summer because they did not have warm clothes to wear.

During this cold season the poor people of 'Akká would gather at one of the clothing shops and 'Abdu'l-Bahá would give each one a cloak to wear. 'Abdu'l-Bahá would put the cloak on many of the poor Himself, especially the most disabled, adjusting the cloak with His own hands and stroking it approvingly, as if to say, 'There! Now you will do well.'

At this time there were five or six hundred poor people in 'Akká and 'Abdu'l-Bahá would give them all a warm piece of clothing each year.

On feast days He would visit the poor at their homes. He would talk with them, ask about their health and comfort, and leave gifts for everyone.[33]

12

SELFLESSNESS

O Lord! Unto Thee I repair for refuge, and toward all Thy signs I set my heart.

O Lord! Whether travelling or at home, and in my occupation or in my work, I place my whole trust in Thee.

Grant me then Thy sufficing help so as to make me independent of all things, O Thou Who art unsurpassed in Thy mercy!

Bestow upon me my portion, O Lord, as Thou pleasest, and cause me to be satisfied with whatsoever Thou hast ordained for me.

Thine is the absolute authority to command.[34]

He is the true servant of God who, in this day, were he to pass through cities of silver and gold, would not deign to look upon them, and whose heart would remain pure and undefiled from whatever things can be seen in this world, be they its goods or its treasures.[35]

A New Car

'Abdu'l-Bahá was almost 70 years old when He decided to travel to Europe and America to tell people about Bahá'u'lláh's plan for love and peace. It was a hard trip for a man so old, who had spent many years of His life in prison.

As He travelled, people came to love Him very much. And they loved what He was doing to help the world.

One day when He was in London a woman came to Him and happily handed Him a cheque.

'I have here a cheque for you from a friend so you can buy a good car to help you with your work in England and Europe,' she said.

'I accept with grateful thanks the gift of your friend,' 'Abdu'l-Bahá said kindly.

He took the cheque in both hands and seemed to bless it.

'I return it to be used for gifts to the poor,' 'Abdu'l-Bahá said as He handed the cheque back to the lady.[36]

13

COURTESY

O Peerless Lord! Be Thou a shelter for this poor child and a kind and forgiving Master unto this erring and unhappy soul. O Lord! Though we are but worthless plants, yet we belong to Thy garden of roses. Though saplings without leaves and blossoms, yet we are a part of Thine orchard. Nurture this plant then through the outpourings of the clouds of Thy tender mercy and quicken and refresh this sapling through the reviving breath of Thy spiritual springtime. Suffer him to become heedful, discerning and noble, and grant that he may attain eternal life and abide in Thy Kingdom for evermore.[37]

We, verily, have chosen courtesy, and made it the true mark of such as are nigh unto Him. Courtesy is, in truth, a raiment which fitteth all men, whether young or old. Well is it with him that adorneth his temple therewith, and woe unto him who is deprived of this great bounty.[38]

No Appointment

When 'Abdu'l-Bahá travelled to the West many people came every day to receive a share of His loving-kindness and listen to His words of wisdom.

When He was in London many people wanted to meet 'Abdu'l-Bahá privately, so it was decided that everyone should make an appointment to see Him.

One day a woman arrived without an appointment. She longed to speak to 'Abdu'l-Bahá.

'Have you an appointment?' asked the person who met her in the hall.

'Alas! No,' she replied.

'I am sorry but He is occupied now with most important people, and cannot be disturbed.'

The woman turned away, bitterly disappointed. She slowly walked down the hall. But before she had reached the foot of the stairway, she was overtaken by a breathless messenger from 'Abdu'l-Bahá.

'He wishes to see you, come back! He has told me to bring you to Him.'

'Abdu'l-Bahá's voice could be heard from the door of His audience room:

'A heart has been hurt. Hasten, hasten, bring her to Me!'[39]

14
LOVING-KINDNESS

O Lord! I am a child; enable me to grow beneath the shadow of Thy loving-kindness. I am a tender plant; cause me to be nurtured through the outpourings of the clouds of Thy bounty. I am a sapling of the garden of love; make me into a fruitful tree.

Thou art the Mighty and the Powerful, and Thou art the All-Loving, the All-Knowing, the All-Seeing.[40]

Do not be content with showing friendship in words alone, let your heart burn with loving kindness for all who may cross your path.[41]

Fruitful Trees

'Abdu'l-Bahá was in London on His way to a meeting where nearly 60 mothers and over one hundred children were gathered. Because they were so poor, they were being looked after by a charity.

When 'Abdu'l-Bahá entered the room, He walked among the women and children, beaming with happiness.

'I am very glad to be among you who are blessed in God's name with children,' He said. 'These little ones will grow to be fruitful trees . . .'

'Abdu'l-Bahá spoke to every child, even the youngest baby, and He gave them all a silver coin. None of the babies cried and everyone felt loved and peaceful.[42]

15

DIVINITY

O Thou pure God! Let these saplings which have sprouted by the stream of Thy guidance become fresh and verdant through the outpourings of the clouds of Thy tender mercy; cause them to be stirred by the gentle winds wafting from the meads of Thy oneness and suffer them to be revived through the rays of the Sun of Reality, that they may continually grow and flourish, and burst into blossoms and fruit.

O Lord God! Bestow upon each one understanding; give them power and strength and cause them to mirror forth Thy divine aid and confirmation, so that they may become highly distinguished among the people.

Thou art the Mighty and the Powerful.[43]

O Befriended Stranger! The candle of thine heart is lighted by the hand of My power, quench it not with the contrary winds of self and passion. The healer of all thine ills is remembrance of Me, forget it not. Make My love thy treasure and cherish it even as thy very sight and life.[44]

Power Within

One day after a meeting in London 'Abdu'l-Bahá arrived home very tired. As usual, many people gathered around Him when He came home. Everyone was sad to see how tired He was and wished He did not have to climb so many stairs to the apartment.

Suddenly, 'Abdu'l-Bahá ran to the top of the stairs without stopping. He looked down at everyone as they walked up after Him. He had a bright smile on His face and all His tiredness had vanished.

'You are all very old! I am very young!' 'Abdu'l-Bahá said. 'Through the power of Bahá'u'lláh all things can be done. I have just used that power.'[45]

16

HUMBLENESS

I am, O my God, but a tiny seed which Thou hast sown in the soil of Thy love, and caused to spring forth by the hand of Thy bounty. This seed craveth, therefore, in its inmost being, for the waters of Thy mercy and the living fountain of Thy grace. Send down upon it, from the heaven of Thy loving-kindness, that which will enable it to flourish beneath Thy shadow and within the borders of Thy court. Thou art He Who watereth the hearts of all that have recognized Thee from Thy plenteous stream and the fountain of Thy living waters.

Praised be God, the Lord of the worlds.[46]

O Son of Man! Humble thyself before Me, that I may graciously visit thee. Arise for the triumph of My cause, that while yet on earth thou mayest obtain the victory.[47]

Crystal Water

When 'Abdu'l-Bahá was visiting America some wealthy friends made a complicated plan for Him to wash His hands before eating a meal. They arranged for a specially dressed boy to carry a colourful bowl with 'crystal water' inside and had a perfumed towel ready for Him to dry His hands.

'Abdu'l-Bahá was in the garden and saw the group of friends with the little boy, the bowl and the towel coming towards Him from across the lawn. He knew why they were approaching Him. Quickly He found some water nearby, washed His hands and dried them with a piece of cloth from the gardener. Radiantly, He then turned to greet the friends and asked them to use the water and towel to wash their own hands instead.[48]

17

JOY

O Lord! Make these children excellent plants. Let them grow and develop in the Garden of Thy Covenant, and bestow freshness and beauty through the outpourings from the clouds of the all-glorious Kingdom.

O Thou kind Lord! I am a little child, exalt me by admitting me to the kingdom. I am earthly, make me heavenly; I am of the world below, let me belong to the realm above; gloomy, suffer me to become radiant; material, make me spiritual, and grant that I may manifest Thine infinite bounties.

Thou art the Powerful, the All-Loving.[49]

Tell thou of abiding joy and spiritual delights, and godlike qualities, and of how the Sun of Truth hath risen above the earth's horizons: tell of the blowing of the spirit of life into the body of the world.[50]

Finding Laughter

In August 1912 when 'Abdu'l-Bahá was in the United States He visited the home of Mrs Parsons, a devoted Bahá'í. Mrs Parsons had a large estate and during the summer many important people would visit her. One day she organized a lunch party at her home and asked 20 people to come and meet 'Abdu'l-Bahá. Each person invited was outstanding in a different area of life – culture, science, art, wealth, politics and achievement. Mrs Parsons was eager for 'Abdu'l-Bahá to tell these influential people about Bahá'u'lláh and His message for mankind.

The guests might have thought they were in for a long lecture but instead 'Abdu'l-Bahá told them a story which made them laugh. He also laughed enthusiastically. Then, encouraged by His story, they told their own funny stories. They were full of joy while they ate their lunch.

'It is good to laugh,' 'Abdu'l-Bahá said, 'laughter is a spiritual relaxation.'

'Abdu'l-Bahá then talked about the years He spent in prison in 'Akká. He explained that life was hard and full of difficulties but at the end of each day they would sit together and talk about the fantastic events of the day and laugh over them. There were not a lot of funny things that happened in a day in prison but they would search hard to find them and laugh about them.

'Abdu'l-Bahá told them joy is not only for people who live in material comfort. Otherwise, unhappiness would have ruled every hour of their days in 'Akká.

The guests looked at 'Abdu'l-Bahá with deep admiration and respect.[51]

18
CHARITY

Verily Thy lovers thirst, O my Lord; lead them to the wellspring of bounty and grace. Verily, they hunger; send down unto them Thy heavenly table . . .

    Heroes are they, O my Lord, lead them to the field of battle. Guides are they, make them to speak out with arguments and proofs. Ministering servants are they, cause them to pass round the cup that brimmeth with the wine of certitude. O my God, make them to be songsters that carol in fair gardens, make them lions that couch in the thickets, whales that plunge in the vasty deep.

    Verily, Thou art He of abounding grace. There is none other God save Thee, the Mighty, the Powerful, the Ever-Bestowing.[52]

For in its teachings we seek the spirit of charity and love to bind the hearts of men together.[53]

Christmas Eve

On Christmas Eve in 1912 'Abdu'l-Bahá went to the Salvation Army Shelter in London. There were a thousand homeless men eating a special Christmas dinner. 'Abdu'l-Bahá spoke to them while they ate. He reminded them that Jesus had been poor and it was easier for the poor than the rich to enter the Kingdom of Heaven. The men sat enchanted by 'Abdu'l-Bahá and what He had to say. Some were in such awe they forgot to eat, even though they were hungry.

As 'Abdu'l-Bahá was leaving He gave the Shelter money to buy a similar dinner for everyone on New Year's Eve. The men, hearing of 'Abdu'l-Bahá's generosity, stood up and cheered Him as He left, waving their knives and forks in the air.[54]

19
HUMILITY

O God! O God! Thou seest my weakness, lowliness and humility before Thy creatures; nevertheless, I have trusted in Thee and have arisen in the promotion of Thy teachings among Thy strong servants, relying on Thy power and might.

O Lord! I am a broken-winged bird and desire to soar in Thy limitless space. How is it possible for me to do this save through Thy providence and grace, Thy confirmation and assistance.

O Lord! Have pity on my weakness, and strengthen me with Thy power. O Lord! Have pity on my impotence, and assist me with Thy might and majesty . . .

Verily, Thou art the Clement, the Powerful, the Mighty, and the Most Merciful of the merciful.[55]

The teacher should not see in himself any superiority; he should speak with the utmost kindliness, lowliness and humility, for such speech exerteth influence and educateth the souls.[56]

'Abdu'l-Bahá Becomes a Knight

A blockade was set up during World War I to stop armed forces from coming into Haifa. This made it very difficult to get food into Haifa. 'Abdu'l-Bahá had in 1912 begun preparing for the war by arranging for wheat to be grown on Bahá'í land near Tiberias. Food was stored in underground pits. During the war He distributed the food to the people of Haifa regardless of their religion or culture. The food was carefully rationed and 'Abdu'l-Bahá saved many people from starvation.

When the war ended the British realized what 'Abdu'l-Bahá had done for the people of Haifa. They wanted to honour Him by making Him a knight.

'Abdu'l-Bahá agreed to accept the knighthood but He was not impressed with worldly honours and ceremonies. He was to be knighted on 27 April 1920 at the home of the British Governor in Haifa. On that day an elegant car was sent to bring Him to the Governor's house.

Isfandíyár, 'Abdu'l-Bahá's long-time faithful servant, stood near by. Many times Isfandíyár had accompanied 'Abdu'l-Bahá on His outings, but seeing the elegant car, he felt sad and unneeded. 'Abdu'l-Bahá sensed how Isfandíyár felt and signalled to him. Isfandíyár ran off and returned with the usual horse-drawn carriage. Isfandíyár was very happy to know he was still needed and drove 'Abdu'l-Bahá to the Governor's house.

There a special ceremony was held for 'Abdu'l-Bahá. British and religious dignitaries came to pay tribute to Him. 'Abdu'l-Bahá's unselfish acts had won Him the love and respect of all types of people.

'Abdu'l-Bahá was knighted Sir 'Abdu'l-Bahá 'Abbás, KBE – a title He never used.[57]

BIBLIOGRAPHY

Abdul Baha on Divine Philosophy. Boston: The Tudor Press, 1918.

'Abdu'l-Bahá. *Paris Talks*. London: Bahá'í Publishing Trust, 1967.

— *The Promulgation of Universal Peace*. Wilmette, IL: Bahá'í Publishing Trust, 1982.

— *Selections from the Writings of 'Abdu'l-Bahá*. Haifa: Bahá'í World Centre, 1978.

— *Tablets of Abdul-Baha Abbas*. New York: Bahá'í Publishing Committee; vol. 1, 1930; vol. 2, 1940; vol. 3, 1930.

Bahá'í Prayers: A Selection of Prayers revealed by Bahá'u'lláh, the Báb and 'Abdu'l-Bahá. Wilmette, IL: Bahá'í Publishing Trust, 2002.

Bahá'u'lláh. *Epistle to the Son of the Wolf*. Wilmette, IL: Bahá'í Publishing Trust, 1988.

— *The Hidden Words*. Wilmette, IL: Bahá'í Publishing Trust, 1990.

— *Prayers and Meditations*. Wilmette, IL: Bahá'í Publishing Trust, 1987.

Balyuzi, H. M. *'Abdu'l-Bahá: The Centre of the Covenant of Bahá'u'lláh*. Oxford: George Ronald, 2nd ed. with minor corr. 1987.

— *Bahá'u'lláh: The King of Glory*. Oxford: George Ronald, 1980.

Blomfield, Lady [Sitárih Khánum; Sara Louise]. *The Chosen Highway*. Oxford: George Ronald, rpt. 2007.

The Compilation of Compilations. Prepared by the Universal House of Justice 1963–1990. 2 vols. [Mona Vale NSW]: Bahá'í Publications Australia, 1991.

Dayspring Magazine, issue 63. National Spiritual Assembly of the United Kingdom.

Honnold, Annamarie. *Vignettes from the Life of 'Abdu'l-Bahá*. Oxford: George Ronald, rev. ed. 1991.

Let Thy Breeze Refresh Them: Bahá'í Prayers and Tablets for Children. Oakham: Bahá'í Publishing Trust, 1976.

Mehrabi, Jacqueline. *Stories of 'Abdu'l-Bahá*. London: Bahá'í Publishing Trust, 1984.

Phelps, Myron H. *The Master in 'Akká*. Los Angeles: Kalimát Press, 1985.

Ruhi Institute. *Teaching Children's Classes, Grade 1*. West Palm Beach, FL: Palabra Publications, 1995.

Shoghi Effendi. *God Passes By*. Wilmette, IL: Bahá'í Publishing Trust, rev. ed. 1995.

Taafaki, Irene. *Thoughts: Education for Peace and One World*. Oxford: George Ronald, 1986.

REFERENCES

i. 'Abdu'l-Bahá, *Tablets*, vol. 2, p. 430.
ii. ibid.
1. The Báb, *Bahá'í Prayers*, p. 56.
2. Bahá'u'lláh, *Hidden Words*, Arabic no. 53.
3. Adapted by Munirih Hodge from Balyuzi, *'Abdu'l-Bahá*, p. 9.
4. 'Abdu'l-Bahá, in *Bahá'í Prayers*, pp. 33–4.
5. Bahá'u'lláh, *Hidden Words*, Arabic no. 7.
6. Adapted by Munirih Hodge from Balyuzi, *'Abdu'l-Bahá*, pp. 11–12.
7. 'Abdu'l-Bahá, *Selections*, pp. 222–3.
8. ibid. p. 228.
9. Adapted by Munirih Hodge from Phelps, *Master in 'Akká*, pp. 25–30.
10. Bahá'u'lláh, *Prayers and Meditations*, pp. 312–13.
11. 'Abdu'l-Bahá, *Selections*, pp. 197–8.
12. Adapted by Munirih Hodge from Phelps, *Master in 'Akká*, pp. 35–41; Shoghi Effendi, *God Passes By*, p. 131; and Balyuzi, *King of Glory*, p. 154.
13. Bahá'u'lláh, *Prayers and Meditations*, pp. 53–4.
14. 'Abdu'l-Bahá, *Selections*, p. 85.
15. Adapted by Munirih Hodge from Shoghi Effendi, *God Passes By*, p. 180; Balyuzi, *'Abdu'l-Bahá*, pp. 20–5; and Phelps, *Master in 'Akká*, pp. 75–85.
16. Bahá'u'lláh, *Prayers and Meditations*, pp. 158–9.
17. Bahá'u'lláh, *Hidden Words*, Arabic no. 48.
18. Adapted by Munirih Hodge from Phelps, *Master in 'Akká*, pp. 101–3.
19. 'Abdu'l-Bahá, in *Bahá'í Prayers*, p. 112.
20. 'Abdu'l-Bahá, *Selections*, p. 201.
21. Adapted by Munirih Hodge from Mehrabi, *Stories of 'Abdu'l-Bahá*, p. 21.
22. 'Abdu'l-Bahá, in *Bahá'í Prayers*, pp. 87–8.
23. 'Abdu'l-Bahá, *Selections*, p. 294.
24. Adapted by Munirih Hodge from Honnold, *Vignettes*, pp. 36–7.
25. 'Abdu'l-Bahá, in *Bahá'í Prayers*, p. 71.
26. 'Abdu'l-Bahá, in *Divine Philosophy*, pp. 41–2.
27. Adapted by Munirih Hodge from Honnold, *Vignettes*, p. 66.
28. 'Abdu'l-Bahá, in *Bahá'í Prayers*, p. 28.
29. 'Abdu'l-Bahá, *Selections*, p. 3.
30. Adapted by Munirih Hodge from Honnold, *Vignettes*, pp. 66–7.
31. 'Abdu'l-Bahá, in *Bahá'í Prayers*, pp. 112–13.
32. Bahá'u'lláh, *Hidden Words*, Arabic no. 30.
33. Adapted by Munirih Hodge from Taafaki, *Thoughts*, p. 240.
34. The Báb, in *Bahá'í Prayers*, pp. 55–6.
35. Bahá'u'lláh, quoted in *Compilation*, vol. 2, p. 330.
36. Adapted by Munirih Hodge from Taafaki, *Thoughts*, pp. 97–8.
37. 'Abdu'l-Bahá, in *Bahá'í Prayers*, pp. 30–1.
38. Bahá'u'lláh, *Epistle*, p. 50.

39. Adapted by Munirih Hodge from Blomfield, *Chosen Highway*, p. 159.
40. 'Abdu'l-Bahá, in *Bahá'í Prayers*, pp. 31–2.
41. 'Abdu'l-Bahá, *Paris Talks*, p. 16.
42. From *Dayspring* Magazine, issue 63, p. 5.
43. 'Abdu'l-Bahá, in *Let Thy Breeze Refresh Them* . . .
44. Bahá'u'lláh, *Hidden Words*, Persian no. 32.
45. Adapted by Munirih Hodge from Blomfield, *Chosen Highway*, p. 169.
46. Bahá'u'lláh, in *Bahá'í Prayers*, p. 172.
47. Bahá'u'lláh, *Hidden Words*, Arabic no. 42.
48. Adapted by Munirih Hodge from Ruhi Institute, *Teaching Children's Classes*, p. 55.
49. 'Abdu'l-Bahá, in *Bahá'í Prayers*, pp. 28-29.
50. 'Abdu'l-Bahá, *Selections*, pp. 92–3.
51. Adapted by Munirih Hodge from Balyuzi, *'Abdu'l-Bahá*, pp. 31–2.
52. 'Abdu'l-Bahá, *Selections*, pp. 224–5.
53. 'Abdu'l-Bahá, *Promulgation*, p. 328.
54. Adapted by Munirih Hodge from Honnold, *Vignettes*, p. 78.
55. 'Abdu'l-Bahá, in *Bahá'í Prayers*, pp. 207–9.
56. 'Abdu'l-Bahá, *Selections*, p. 30.
57. Adapted by Munirih Hodge from Honnold, *Vignettes*, pp. 17–18.